STARTERS
LONG AGO
BOOKS

Stone Age Men

Macdonald Educational

These Stone Age men are hunting for food.
They chase a stag.

Stone Age people lived thousands of years ago.
The men hunted the food.
The women worked at home.
Their home was often a cave.

These men chased a sabre-tooth tiger.
The tiger was very fierce.
It had long teeth like swords.

4

pit

stakes

foliage

stake

The men had dug a pit.
They chased the tiger into the hidden pit.
The tiger fell onto the sharp stakes in it.

Here is a mammoth.
A mammoth was a hairy elephant.
Stone Age men were frightened of mammoths.

flint seam

bone shovel

Flint is a kind of stone.
These men are mining flint.
Stone Age men found out
how to make tools from flints.

chipped flint tools

This Stone Age man is making flint tools.
He chips at the flint with another stone.
This gives the flint a sharp edge.

1. Chipping the flint.

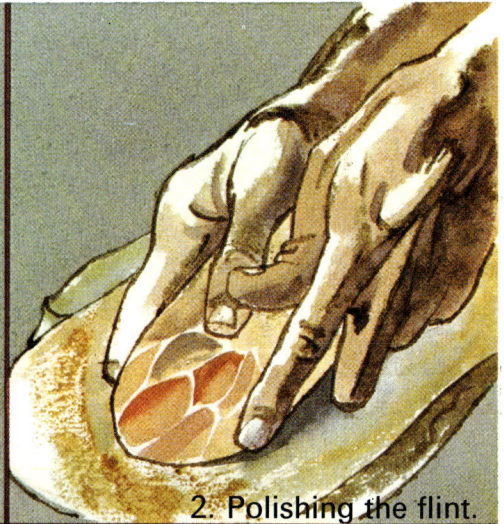

2. Polishing the flint.

3. Sharpening the edge.

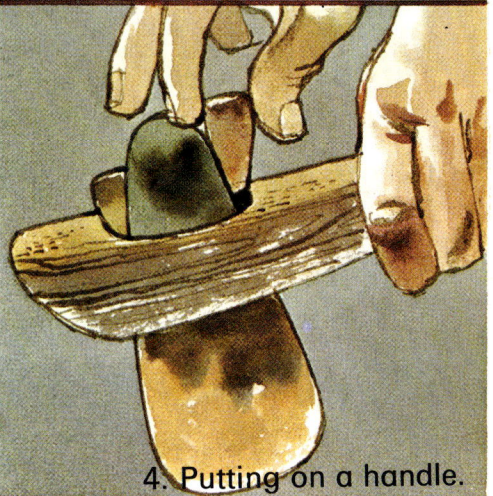

4. Putting on a handle.

Later Stone Age men made elaborate tools.
The pictures show how they made an axe.
They also put on a handle.

skin clothes

skin tent

scraper

skin

This woman is cleaning a leather skin.
She used a scraper made from flint.
She made clothes and tents from leather.

10

This man used flint to make a fire.
He struck the flint against stone
until it made a spark.
The spark set the leaves alight.

Here is a family in a cave.
The cave was their home.
It was safe and warm inside.

12

There was always a fire in the cave.
It kept them warm.
It gave them light.
It frightened wild animals away.

These men came to find a new cave for a home.
But a bear already lived in this cave.
The bear fought with them for the cave.

twig brush

bone palette

Stone Age men did paintings on cave walls.
The paintings were a kind of magic.
The men painted the animals
they wanted to catch.

harpoon

Here is a man fishing in the river.
He used a harpoon.
He speared the fish with the harpoon.

16

There is a boat on the river.
Some men are making another boat.
They dig out a hollow in a tree trunk.

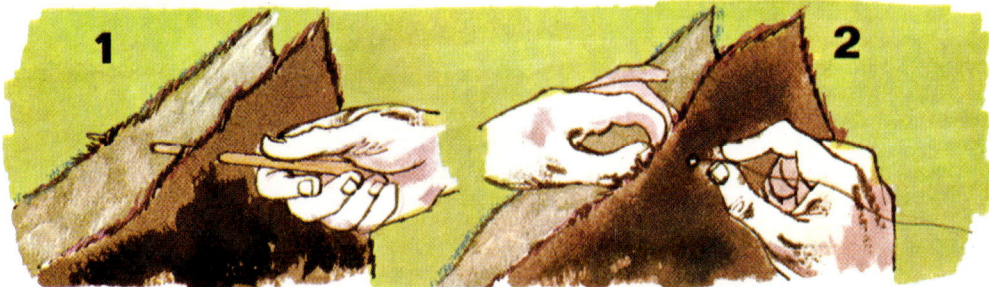

1. They punched a hole, then pushed the thread through.

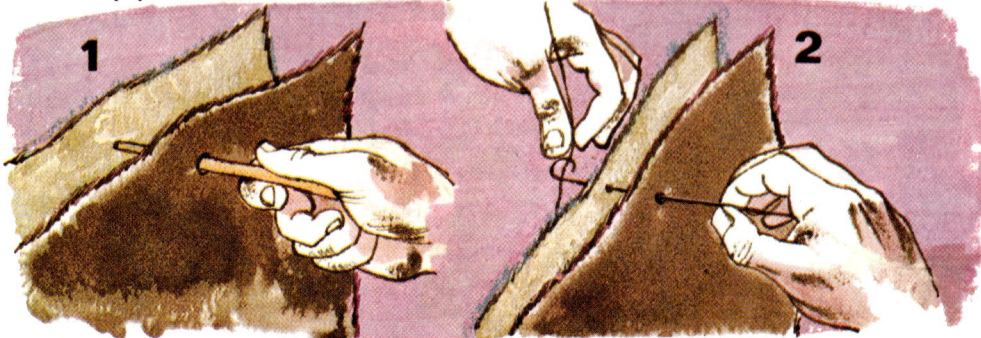

2. They punched a hole, then hooked the thread through.

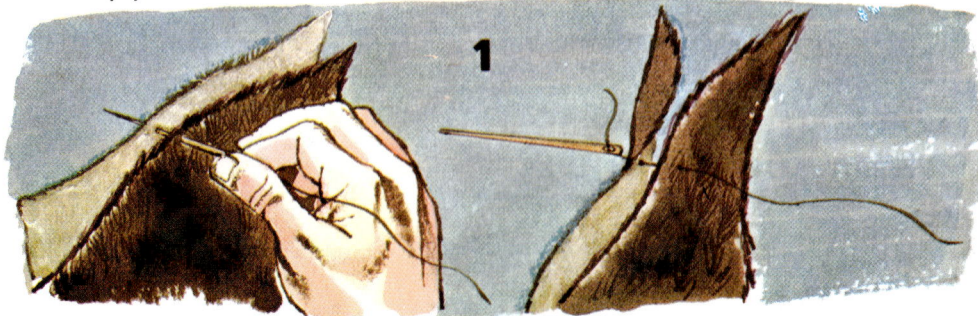

3. They used a needle to make a hole and pull the thread through.

Stone Age women learned to sew.
The pictures show how they discovered sewing.
The last picture shows a needle.
The women made the needle from a bone.

This is how thread was made.
The man twisted the wool into thread.
This is called spinning.

1. Mixing the clay.

2. Coiling the pot.

3. Drying the first half.

4. Coiling the bottom half.

5. Closing the hole
   in the bottom of the pot.

6. Baking pots to dry them
   and make them hard.

This is how Stone Age women made pots.
They mixed clay and sand.
They coiled this into pots and baked them dry.

oven

They used clay to make ovens too.
This woman will cook the food
in the clay oven.

reaping the corn

Here are some Stone Age farmers.
They are working in the field.
Stone Age farmers grew crops
and kept tame animals.

grinding
flour

milking the goat

The farmers lived in a village.
The houses were made of wood.
One woman is grinding corn into flour.
She will make bread from the flour.

lintel

upright

Sometimes Stone Age men built temples of stone.
They built them for their gods.

1. Levering the upright into the pit.

2. Pulling up the upright.

3. Levering up the lintel.

4. Supporting the lintel before levering it again.

Stone Age men had no machines
to help them build.
They probably built the pillars like this.

1. Roll the clay into coils.

2. Lay the coils in circles
   like this to make a pot.

See if you can make some pots.
Make them in clay,
like New Stone Age men did.

3. Push the clay coils together with your thumb.

4. Smooth the pot with the back of a spoon.

5. You can leave it to dry.

6. Or you can ask your teacher to help you fire it in a bonfire.

You can leave your pots
to dry in the sun.
Or ask your teacher to help you
fire them in a bonfire.

Index